Royal Heritage Series

The Story
of
PRINCE ANDREW

Text by TREVOR HALL

Produced by Ted Smart and David Gibbon

COLOUR LIBRARY BOOKS

"The Queen has collywobbles," trumpeted the newspapers in July 1959. It was a diagnosis from a distance, the last and silliest in a long line of offerings to a public whose curiosity and concern had been aroused by their sovereign's undisputed listlessness during a busy tour of Canada. Everything from strain to a chill had been suggested as its cause, but the ubiquitous Palace spokesman denied them all. Nobody seemed to know what collywobbles were, but they seemed to fill the explanatory void. As W.S. Gilbert wrote, the meaning doesn't matter if it's only idle chatter . . .

Those famous collywobbles turned out to be the beginnings of the man we now know as Prince Andrew. By the end of the first week in August, Britain was jubilant with the realisation that, after a child-free hiatus of nine years, the Queen was expecting her third child. The phrase itself was almost lèse-majesté, sounding too abruptly physical by half to be applied to the delicate intimacies of royal private life. But the knowledge that the baby would be the first born to a reigning sovereign for 103 years conferred a nobility upon the plain fact, as if the Queen were acting out some ritualistic sacrifice to history.

In today's liberated, questioning and cynical world, the attitudes surrounding the event seem Victorian. Indeed Prince Andrew's own recent escapades, combining the quest for fun with the tinge of scandal, render them almost medieval. That is no more than a sign of the speed at which the transformations in popular outlook have taken place, and for the British monarchy that has meant accepting familiarity in place of reverence, scepticism in place of awe, sincerity in place of sycophancy. Those changes ran parallel with Prince Andrew's own life, which began on the afternoon of 19th February, 1960. Luckily for him, he was subjected to them only insofar as the expertly-controlled programme for his exposure to the world around him would allow. And for the first eight years of his life, that meant watching the world progress from the privileged security of a quartet of historic royal residences, without suffering the indignities and assaults of its growing brashness and curiosity.

That of course had been so for Prince Charles. But his upbringing had been unavoidably jaundiced, when he was only three, by the irrevocable step he took nearer the Throne on the death of his grandfather. The "ghastly inexorable sense" with which he realised his position was understandable. Second in line is not so bad, though recent royal history suggests it is no guarantee either. But somehow, one cannot imagine Prince Andrew regarding his destiny with such morose alarm. He was from the start an outgoing, extrovert lad, active where Charles had been contemplative, grinning where the elder brother had frowned, confident rather than uncertain. The photographs, and they soon accumulated in scrapbooks and magazines throughout the country, said it all. So much so that what had seemed a bold experiment when Prince Charles was first sent to school, now seemed the natural course for the education of princes. Andrew tumbled into school existence from the age of eight as if he had been waiting for it all his life. Gregarious, mischievous, inquiring and above all sporting, he nailed the myth of royal apartheid for good. What had seemed unthinkable only a quarter of a century before was now regarded as common practice. It was those changing attitudes again.

His transfer to Gordonstoun at the age of thirteen was as inevitable as was the co-educational development of the school, or as his reputation as a ladies' man. By the age of sixteen he had developed a powerful physique and darkish good looks sufficient to meet the modern film star requirement. If Prince Charles didn't refer to him once as "the one with the Robert Redford looks," he should have. Before Andrew realised it himself, he was being branded as everything short of a latter day Casanova. Any girl he spoke to at school was, if the story reached the press, a fair candidate for the next royal tiara. At Lakefield, the Canadian college where he spent half of 1977, the more relaxed atmosphere made chance meetings with the opposite sex a daily occurrence, and his reputation lost none of its *élan*. If anything, life in the Royal Navy has made it worse. Though not yet accused of having "a girl in every port," his shore leaves are watched avidly for the day when it might be true. He is fair game for the gossips, and Koo Stark is perhaps only the beginning. Indeed, as Prince Andrew has just emerged into anything like a truly public life, this story itself is only the beginning. Marriage, a dukedom, children, a career of ribbon-cutting and stone-laying – all lie ahead. The consequences, and how he faces them, may all depend on the influences of the last twenty-three years – the story so far.

Andrew Albert Christian Edward were the names given to the first baby to be born to a reigning monarch since Princess Beatrice in 1857. They were family names of course, and it was in the bosom of his family that the young Prince Andrew was most frequently seen in his early years. Trooping the Colour provided the best opportunities, but those who carefully followed the

movements of the Queen and her family in their less official activities could see the growing Prince being carried, later toddling, later still confidently striding on and off trains at Euston, King's Cross or Liverpool Street as his parents, grandmother, brother, sister and cousins were reunited for holidays at Balmoral or Sandringham. Indeed, 1960 was very much a family year. Only a week after his birth, his aunt Princess Margaret announced her engagement to Antony Armstrong-Jones, though Andrew was much too young to attend their wedding that May. In August the Queen Mother celebrated her sixtieth birthday and as a special treat Andrew was sent to Clarence House so that he

could be photographed on his grandmother's knee. Over the years, many official photographs were to be released, emphasising the pride which his busy parents took in their third child, and making no concession to Andrew's own inevitable future as the second son of the sovereign.

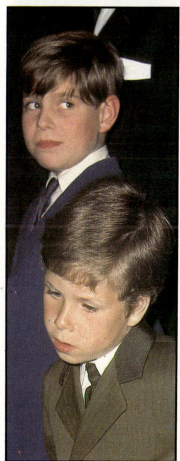

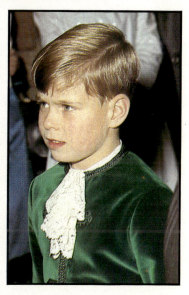

His introduction to the public was gradual. He was soon in great demand as a page-boy at family weddings, like that of the Marquis of Hamilton in October 1966 (above). One of his first introductions to modern technology occurred almost two years later (left) when, with his young cousin Viscount Linley, he saw the new

Hovercraft under construction at Cowes. It seemed, in fact, that 1968 was his "coming out" year. By then he was no longer the youngest child, and there was every reason for his being brought on a little more. That year he joined the First Marylebone Cub Scout pack (below) and enjoyed several special outings at Windsor. Among them was a Freedom of Windsor ceremony (far right); many weekends at Smith's Lawn where, sometimes with Lord Mountbatten (opposite page, bottom right), he watched his father play polo, and the Royal Windsor Horse Show in May (bottom right).

Naturally his educational needs emphasised the importance of home life, and holidays began to follow the royal pattern – Easter at Windsor, summer in Scotland, with trips to the Braemar Games in September (top right, in 1968; opposite page, bottom left, in 1969), and New Year at Sandringham (right, in 1969). Christmas at Windsor meant meeting his now numerous cousins: (opposite page, top) after the 1969 Christmas Day service.

Heatherdown does not sound the sort of school to make potential men out of mere boys, but its good reputation and nearness to Windsor made it an appropriate choice for Prince Andrew. In September 1968 he wore a smart, grey suit for his introduction to a school where he would be equal with other boys, and the Headmaster was there to greet the new boy and his distinguished parents. Andrew's five years at Heatherdown were uneventful and unspoilt by publicity. Unlike Prince Charles, he oozed confidence – as the photograph of the family at Sandringham in 1969 (opposite) shows. But, although he excelled at sports, he lacked the academic flair

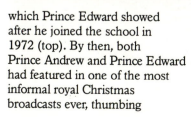

which Prince Edward showed after he joined the school in 1972 (top). By then, both Prince Andrew and Prince Edward had featured in one of the most informal royal Christmas broadcasts ever, thumbing through the pages of the Queen's photograph album (top right), and in official photographs at Balmoral (above) and Buckingham Palace marking their parents' Silver Wedding Anniversary in November 1972.

Prince Andrew followed his father and brother to Gordonstoun School in September 1973. His aptitude for sport and outdoor recreation made him the envy of his counterparts, though in the classroom he was something of a disappointment. By the middle of 1979, however, he had all three A-levels under his belt.

He left Gordonstoun that year and spent summer with his family at Balmoral, where photographs were taken to commemorate the Queen and Prince Philip's 32nd wedding anniversary the following November (opposite page). Prince Andrew was a noticeably different character from the pre-teenager who attended his parents' Silver Wedding Thanksgiving Service seven years earlier (right). In July 1980, he joined his grandmother's 80th birthday celebrations, and was part of the family group surrounding her in the official photographs (above).

The Queen and all her family were, for the first and only time to date, present in Canada simultaneously in 1976. They assembled to watch Princess Anne compete in the Montreal Olympics. For Prince Andrew it was a prelude to a longer visit to Canada, beginning in January 1977, as a student at Lakefield College, Ontario. Here for six months he enriched his love of the outdoors by learning to canoe, kayak, play ice-hockey and ski cross-country.

Prince Andrew's interest in the armed services began while he was still at Gordonstoun. In 1978 he opted for naval flying and a course in parachuting at Brize Norton (above). He confessed nervousness on the day of his first drop (left and opposite): "If you're not nervous," he said, "you'll do something stupid". Watching the showjumping at Badminton (below, in 1981) was less nerve-racking.

Like many Windsors and Mountbattens before him, Andrew Mountbatten-Windsor joined the Royal Navy as a midshipman, enrolling under his commanding officer Captain Nicholas Hunt (below) at Britannia Royal Naval College Dartmouth in August 1979. He was smartly on parade (right, far right and bottom) in March 1980 for his Passing Out ceremony and needless to say, the Queen attended the parade and reviewed the ranks (opposite). At 1981's Trooping (bottom right) he accompanied Lady Diana Spencer, just six weeks before acting as supporter at Prince Charles' wedding (overleaf).

Best Wishes from... the BURNLEY

By the end of 1981, after his final and successfully completed training as an operational and qualified helicopter pilot, Prince Andrew was set to join 820 Helicopter Squadron on board the 19,500-ton submarine-hunter *HMS Invincible* – where these pictures were taken at the time of his homecoming from the Falklands in September 1982. The Queen and Prince Philip arrived with Princess Anne at Portsmouth Dockyard to welcome the confident, and now highly experienced helicopter pilot back from the South Atlantic. From the bobbing barge they climbed up narrow wooden steps

onto *Invincible* and were led to the Admiral's cabin for a private twenty-minute reunion with Prince Andrew.
The Queen, Prince Philip and Princess Anne, having met their own family member and shared in the greetings for a thousand others, left the bustling, noisy harbour and its occupants to the joys of their own reunions. Prince Andrew left with them, but made his way to London for the evening, before returning to Portsmouth to fly his helicopter back to its base at RNAF Culdrose in Cornwall.

After a final tour on *Invincible* ending in 1983, Prince Andrew prepared for a transfer from Culdrose to Portland to join 702 Squadron, training as a Lynx helicopter

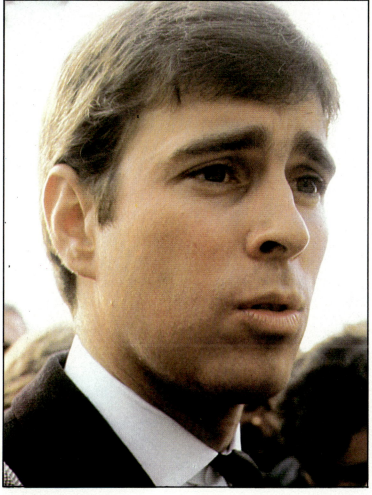

pilot. The days when he used
merely to watch Prince Charles
commanding *HMS Bronington* in
1976 (overleaf, top) or even
play second fiddle to him on
the polo field (bottom, at
Windsor in 1980) must have
seemed a long way off.

Prince Andrew laid his first wreath at the Cenotaph in November 1982. Representing those who had fought in the Falklands, he attached the simple message: "In memory of those who died in the South Atlantic – Andrew". To some, the event marked the beginning of his public life, though the previous December had witnessed his first solo engagement – a dinner (opposite) marking the centenary of Rugby Football matches between Oxford and Cambridge Universities.

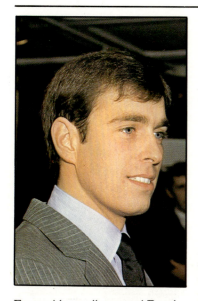

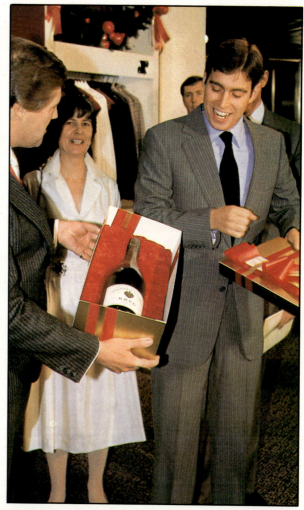

Even with a well-cropped Royal Navy haircut, Prince Andrew lost none of his legendary hold over the girls. It was, nevertheless, strange how, when he merely had eyes for them, he acquired the name Randy Andy, whereas when he was actually seen in their company everyone called him Prince Andrew again. However that may be, when in November 1982 he went to Regent Street to switch on the Christmas illuminations, the girls were ready and waiting to be switched on, too. They screamed like Beatles fans as he arrived, and again as he appeared on a balcony to perform the ceremony. The theme of the illuminations was the Christmas tree. "I'm told there are 55,000 bulbs in those Christmas trees", he said. "I just hope they all work." They all seemed to, as did Prince Andrew's own charm with the lucky shop-assistants he met at a reception afterwards.

Prince Andrew piloted his own helicopter to Biggin Hill to open the International Air Show on 14th May. His tour of the show included watching a Royal Navy rescue demonstration (below) and the manoeuvres of the Harrier jump-jets (bottom right), an inspection of a Flying Fortress aircraft and a look at the cockpit of a World

War II fighter (right and above right). He also obliged those seeking evidence of his stereotype as a man with an eye for the girls, by meeting a line-up of Wrens – one of few meetings with the opposite sex that did not have the newspapers buzzing with speculation. Two of Prince Andrew's first three public engagements of 1983 concerned the armed forces. In July he opened the Fleet Air Arm Museum at Yeovilton.

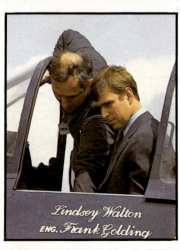

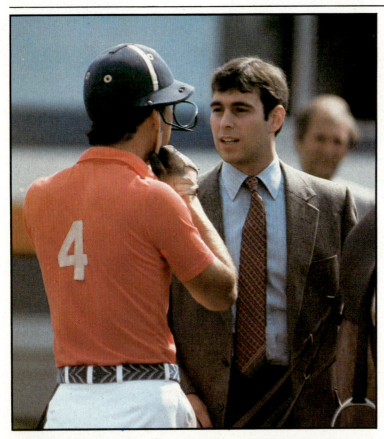

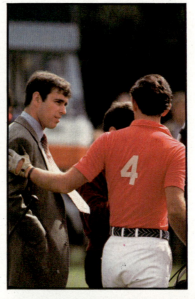

part in them, and is often seen as a spectator at polo matches at Windsor. For Prince Charles that is no bad thing, for if he envies the dash of his younger brother and the sense of adventure and achievement his experience in the Falklands has given him, the polo field is the place to get even. So it was no surprise when the Prince of Wales, securely placed atop his polo pony, indulged in a spot of tomfoolery by prodding Prince Andrew with his polo stick good and hard after Andrew had threatened to yank him off the pony.

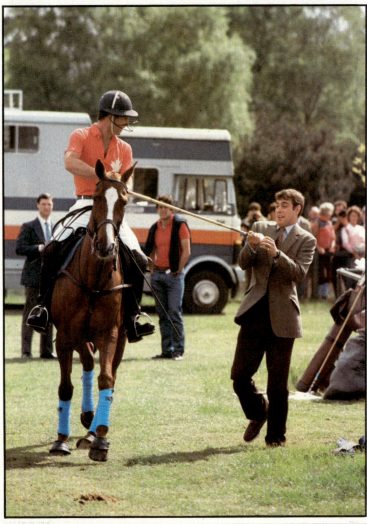

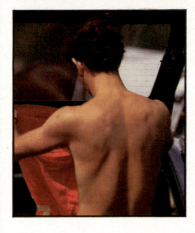

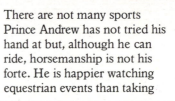

There are not many sports Prince Andrew has not tried his hand at but, although he can ride, horsemanship is not his forte. He is happier watching equestrian events than taking

"Prince Andrew", said the Lord Mayor of Portsmouth, "is already held with affection in the hearts of our citizens through his duties in the Royal Navy". It was also fitting, he added, that "this energetic young man" should be opening a leisure centre on his first official visit to the city. The centre was named in honour of Lord Mountbatten, and the late Earl's grandson Lord Romsey, and Lady Romsey, were there to greet the Prince on his arrival (far right).

Inside the building the Sea Lord Bar and the Lord Louis Suite, perpetuate Mountbatten's memory, and the plaque which Prince Andrew unveiled bore the Mountbatten family coat of arms opposite that of the City of Portsmouth.

Everybody seemed to be studying Prince Andrew's eyes as he watched a display of gymnastics performed by some attractive-looking girls.

Aikido and karate were some of the subsequent features of the display, at the end of which the Prince was presented with a squash racquet – presumably for when he uses the life membership card he received.

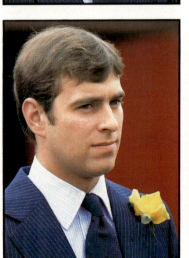

Prince Andrew's long weekend in Newport, Rhode Island, to lend support to Britain's America's Cup challenge began with a reception at the Old Colony House. The smiles wreathing

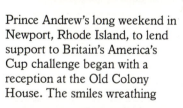

his face hid his understandable concern for his safety as IRA protestors chanted and heckled during his arrival. When a cannon boomed out a gun salute, the Prince jumped, his detective reacted – then both roared with laughter as they

realised their mistake.
The Prince was in Rhode Island
as a guest of Peter de Savary,
the oil and property
millionaire, whose efforts to
win the America's Cup for
Britain have been unsparing.
The British yacht *Victory 83*
had been named by Princess

Michael of Kent in March and both she and Prince Michael had called in on the crew in the Bahamas that month. Prince Andrew, watching from the motor launch *Lisanola* as *Victory 83*

was put through her paces, came even closer and did some sailing on the yacht himself. Later, the Prince visited the Naval War College and had dinner with a party of 120 distinguished guests at a local restaurant before the main event of the weekend – the British Ball at Beechwood. "Who are you taking to the ball?" one journalist had asked him that morning. "Myself", replied the Prince. "You've

heard of blind dates, haven't you?" In the event he was accompanied by the mysterious lady in pink, whose name he refused to divulge as he passed ranks of photographers yelling for details that evening. Once inside, he and his companion split up and the Prince joined in the festivities by dancing with Lana Paton (in blue), the girlfriend of Peter de Savary, whom he thanked afterwards for allowing him to enjoy her company. Tickets for the ball had cost $150, and de Savary had a garden landscaped and a fountain built in the grounds for the occasion at a cost of around $100,000. Among the attractions inside were the band of Her Majesty's Brigade of Guards, Peter Duchin's orchestra, and the Sonatas Steel Band. After the ball, the entire complement of guests went outside to watch Beating

Retreat, and a huge firework display lit up the Newport sky that night.

The remainder of Prince Andrew's official time during the weekend was taken up attending a mayoral reception, and a church service at the Trinity Church. Spare time was spent enjoying the perfect weather in de Savary's yacht *Calysma* and attending a cricket match (these pages) – one of the few examples of the British institution ever staged in the United States.

This four-day visit to the United States was the last of Prince Andrew's few official engagements of the year. There is likely to be only a modest increase in the immediate future, for his eight remaining years of service in the Royal Navy will consume most of his time.

The Queen Mother's Scottish home is the Castle of Mey, the most northerly of Britain's castles, and the pictures (these pages) show the Queen, together with Prince Andrew, Prince Edward, Princess Anne and her children paying one of their customary summer visits to the Queen Mother from the Royal Yacht *Britannia*.

(Above, below and bottom left): the Prince visits the British Airways Helicopters Ltd base at Aberdeen on 16th August, 1983. (Remaining pictures): arriving at the Castle of Mey.

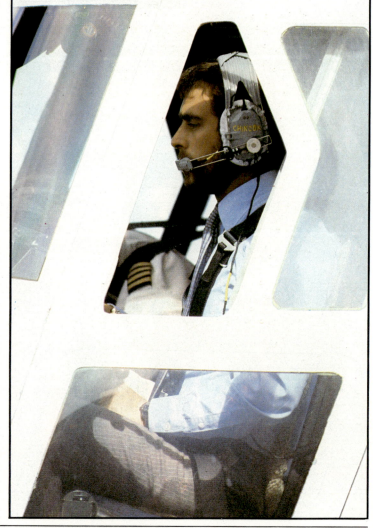

First published in Great Britain by Colour Library Books Ltd.
© 1983 Illustrations: Keystone Press Agency, London.
© 1983 Text: Colour Library Books, Guildford, Surrey, England.
Display and text filmsetting by Acesetters Ltd., Richmond, Surrey, England.
Printed and bound in Barcelona, Spain.
ISBN 0 86283 126 1